FOR SEEING
EYE DOGS ONLY

Robert S Swiatek

FOR SEEING
EYE DOGS ONLY

A book on missing intelligence

BY ROBERT S. SWIATEK

Aventine Press

Published by Aventine Press
1023 4th Ave #204
San Diego CA, 92101
www.aventinepress.com

ISBN: 1-59330-282-7

Printed in the United States of America

Table of Contents

1. Government Decisions..1

2. Wondrous Quotes...13

3. Products..21

4. Sign and Sentences...29

5. Disorder in the Court.......................................41

6. Get Your Award..51

7. Missing Marbles...57

8. Random Stupidity...65

9. Observations..71

10. Young Intelligence...75

11. Criminal Behavior..85

12. Words and Expressions....................................97

13. Some Questions...105

This book is dedicated to all those who voted for George Bush in the 2000 and 2004 elections. If you don't understand this, then I've made my point.

Laughter is the best medicine and it's available even if you don't have health insurance.

INTRODUCTION

A teacher attended a conference in Chicago some time ago. At the end of the week, he got a ride to the airport and flew to Buffalo. Upon his arrival home, he sensed that something was not right. It didn't take him too long to realize that his car was missing. He had left it in the windy city.

While in college, I saw a professor park his convertible in the lot with his top down. This was of the car and not of his head. He was on the way to class, but he stopped and went back to the vehicle. He had forgotten something. He got the briefcase and then proceeded to lock the car.

On another occasion, a guy messed up by locking his keys inside his van. After a while, he managed to get inside the vehicle and get his family out.

As you can tell, this is a book about intelligence, or more specifically, the lack of it around us today. The United States can land a man on the moon but we, the citizens of the country, wind up reading words on the mirrors of our cars that say, "Objects in mirror are closer than they appear!" I found that writing on the passenger mirror, but not on the mirror on the driver's side. How can I be sure that the mirror without these words shows a true picture of things behind the car?

People just don't think. They have been given intellects, but from some of their actions, we have to question when they are going to use them. Individuals may have a high IQ, but they still say and do things that indicate they may not be any smarter than a rutabaga. There may be a silver lining, as they need not worry about ever getting brainwashed! This book will show you many instances of this type of behavior.

Throughout the book, many of the names have been changed to show mercy and spare those involved any embarrassment. The fictitious names should be obvious. At the same time, this replacement of names is also intended to protect the author from litigation. As you can see from reading later chapters, people will sue for anything that you can imagine for bucks, most of which they don't deserve. The more incredible fact is that no matter how ridiculous the lawsuit, they sometimes win the case!

AUTHOR'S NOTE

1
GOVERNMENT DECISIONS

A few years ago I decided to obtain a post office box. I went to the local post office and was handed some paperwork. I hate filling out forms or applications but it didn't appear as though I had any choice. However, on reading the document, I noticed the words,

"Filling out this form is optional."

I was relieved since this meant I would be spared some drudgery. My joy was short-lived as I noticed another comment on the page, which said,

"To procure a P. O. box, you must fill out this form."

Leland H. Gregory III wrote a book in 1997 called *Great Government Goofs*. If you get a chance, I recommend it very highly. It's proof that people in politics do things that normal, rational human beings shouldn't do. You will be shocked and upset, but you should get a good laugh as well. You may also conclude that it's time to elect some new Senators and Representatives! I couldn't help but include some of those events here.

Alaska State Senator M. I. Freezin introduced a bill to make it illegal for a civilian dog to impersonate a police dog.

I wonder if the former can still get work as a private detective!

*****

A new danger has arrived: adversarial soda machines. After individuals who service those devices tried to wrangle a free pop and were disgusted by being shortchanged, they tilted, rocked and shook the machines, which fell on them. Three died and twelve had to be hospitalized. Clashes between the machines and those who just wanted a soda resulted in twenty-four injuries and eight deaths.

Those machines will need a lawyer when it comes to trial time.

*****

According to Common Sense Government in 1995, the Defense Department spends more on procedures for travel ($22.2 billion) than on travel ($2 billion.)

The travel plans should be to Mars, and this department should be sent there.

*****

In 1974, the phrase "For Kids' Sake, Think Toy Safety" was displayed on 80,000 buttons. Unfortunately, they all had to be recalled, as the paint was toxic.

These Toys Rn't for Us.

*****

NASA spent $200,000 to develop a sweet potato that can be grown in outer space.

The aliens prefer mashed potatoes and not yams.

*****

In 1987, Mississippi Representative Shirley L. Pass introduced a bill into the Senate legislature that would give dwarfs permission to use crossbows to hunt deer.

I didn't think those people were lobbyists!

*****

In the 1970s during the energy crisis, Ohio Representative Seymour Cold introduced a bill to eliminate January and February from the calendar, since they are the coldest months.

Does that mean that our Congressmen and Senators in Washington will only get paid for ten months of the year? I like that idea.

*****

Congress allocated $19 million to examine the amount of methane gas emitted from cow flatulence.

I don't think the problem should be blamed on the cows.

*****

Texas State Representative Gerry Mandering introduced a bill that would require anyone who plans to commit a crime to give their would-be victim at least twenty-four hours notice in writing or orally, but only in certain crimes.

Wouldn't that spoil the surprise?

*****

In a similar manner, Oklahoma State Representative Eubie Forewarned introduced a bill that would require men to obtain advance permission from any female with whom they wished to have sexual intercourse.

Would it still be needed if the man owned a few oil wells?

*****

$36,749,000 was added by the House of Representatives for a generic increase for industrial preparedness.

At least they saved some money because they didn't get the name brand item.

*****

In the 1996 budget, Congress approved $1 million for potato research. Since 1983, over $13 million has been appropriated for such research.

I hope none of that was for French Fries.

*****

The expression "Premature impact of an aircraft with terrain" is the politically correct FAA term for an airplane crash.

Can you find the oxymoron above?

*****

The cost for the government to buy a stapler is $54, $4 for the actual item and $50 overhead.

I wonder what the staples cost. I guess we'll be using paperclips.

*****

The U.S. Government has thirty two billion cubic feet of helium stored under twenty square miles of the Texas panhandle in case of blimp warfare. This was from 1929, but during the 1960s Congress decided to renew the reserves and ordered an addition to the stockpile.

I wonder where the blimps are stored.

*****

The Illinois Department of Conservation spent $100,000 to study the contents of owl vomit.

I wonder what they plan to do with that stuff. I have some suggestions!

*****

The Pentagon paid $1676 for a ten-foot aluminum ladder.

They obviously didn't try Home Depot!

*****

The Senate proposed spending $1 million to study brown tree snakes. Oddly enough, the species is only found in Guam, not threatening to humans and can't survive in North America.

They may not be tree snakes, but there's something crawling around in the Senate.

*****

The National Institute on Alcohol Abuse and Alcoholism asked for $102,000 for a project that included an experiment to see if sunfish that drink tequila are more aggressive than sunfish that drink gin.

I thought that sunfish only drank beer.

*****

Pratt and Whitney in 1990 charged the government $999 for ordinary pliers.

I hope that came with a warranty.

*****

Representative Gladys Notmee of Culpepper, Virginia proposed a bill that prohibited dead bodies from being stored where food is served.

That's for all those restaurants that have cadavers on the premises.

*****

The Bureau of Indian Affairs included in their 1992 inventory list $297 million for three chain saws, one typewriter set at $96 million and two typewriters——one at $77 million and the other at $42 million.

Fortunately they got the items on sale!

*****

In 1986, the National Park Service purchased a half-acre of land in southwest DC for $230,000. Two years later, it was discovered they had bought the land in 1914, meaning they already owned it.

I wonder whom they bought it from in 1986.

*****

$107,000 was appropriated by Congress for a project to study the sex life of the Japanese quail.

Was there a similar project for the American quail?

*****

Five million dollars was approved by the Senate to renovate buildings and finish an airplane hangar at Michigan's Wurtswirth Air Force Base. This was after the decision was made to close the facility.

Maybe the government has plans to buy the buildings.

*****

In 1993 NASA shelled out $23 million for a prototype toilet for the space shuttle.

That translates into some really expensive bowel movements!

*****

The Pentagon admitted spending nearly 11 million dollars employing psychics to provide military information.

Don't they trust the CIA?

*****

During the 1980s, efficiency experts saved the Department of Defense between $27 million and $136 million each year. However, the annual cost for these "experts" was between $150 million and $300 million.

Now I know whom to contact to save money!

*****

$100,000 was spent to study why people don't like beets.

They probably aren't cooking them.

*****

The El Paso, Texas City Council approved $112,000 to retain a private security firm. This was used to guard the city's police station.

Talk about one tough town!

*****

In 1985 in the Boise, Idaho mayoral election, four write-in votes were received for Mr. Potato Head.

I didn't even know he was running. He was probably the most qualified candidate.

*****

$11.5 million was appropriated by the House to modernize a power plant at the Philadelphia Naval Yard, which at the time, was scheduled to be closed.

Maybe they're planning to use it for Bingo!

*****

The state of Missouri legislators approved a five pound 1,012 page bill aimed at reducing state paperwork.

It's those Missouri politicians who should be reduced in number.

*****

In the 1996 Federal Budget, $3,750,000 was added by the Senate for "Wood Utilization Research." Since 1985, over $35 million has been funneled into this project.

Speaking of wood, it sounds like the intelligence in the Senate doesn't quite match that of Charlie McCarthy, Edgar Bergen's pal.

*****

The University of Massachusetts received $60,000 in Federal grant money to study Belgian endive.

The grant for the radicchio study was turned down.

*****

Congress approved $34,645,000 for research into screwworms, even though the species has been eliminated from the U.S.

In this case, it sounds like the taxpayer was the one who got screwed.

*****

The United States Postal Service spent $23 million to find out how long it takes for the mail to be delivered.

If Newman is a carrier, it may never get delivered.

*****

One million dollars was spent for a program to study how to safely cross the street.

Somehow I think a chicken is involved in this!

*****

This comes from the Buffalo News of Sunday, August 1, 2004.

The charity that runs the Statue of Liberty and Ellis Island is being asked by Congress to explain some of its expenses, including high salaries for its executives and $45,000 a year for a dog that chases away geese.

It wouldn't have been so pricey except he has a pedigree.

*****

When NASA first started sending up astronauts, they quickly discovered that ballpoint pens would not work in zero gravity.

To combat this problem, NASA scientists spent a decade and 12 billion dollars developing a pen that writes in zero gravity, upside down, underwater, on almost any surface including glass and at temperatures ranging from below freezing to over 300° C.

The Russians used a pencil.

*****

The following happened to me recently.

Not long ago I had to drop a document to be copied at an office in Williamsville. I had the option of sending it and having it returned, but then I never would have had this incident to relate. I entered the office and saw a sign instructing me to take a number and have a seat. I also saw another directive to line up behind a certain point. So now, what do I do, take a seat or line up? I took the ticket, which had the number 89 on it and sat down. The number being serviced was 72. There were two clerks working on these numbers.

Not long after I was seated, I saw a customer walk into the office and get taken care of without taking a ticket. I thought maybe I could avoid the long wait and do the same. I asked the guard and he just told me to wait. There was another sign that said that you should take a ticket and wait even if you had an appointment. Every so often, the door would open and the clerk would call out a name. People would then follow that person through the door to a desk. I also noticed that people entered the premises, didn't take a ticket, their names were called and they were escorted to someone's desk. How did the clerk know their names? Why didn't these individuals take tickets? Finally my number came up and I was taken care of in less than three minutes. Nonetheless, I was wondering about a few things. I couldn't figure out what the whole procedure was at this place. Maybe I was trying to be logical and think things out, something I probably shouldn't have been doing. After all, this was a social security office of the United States Government!

*****

I close with something I used in my first book, *The "Read My Lips" Cookbook*. You can find more information on my website, WWW.BOBCOOKS.COM.

"Your food stamps will be stopped effective March 1992 because we received notice that you passed away. May God bless you. You may reapply if there is a change in your circumstances."

——Excerpted from a letter to a dead person from the Greenville County (South Carolina) Department of Social Services.

*****

2
WONDROUS QUOTES

Some people speak for hours and don't say a thing. Others utter statements that aren't completely true. For me to include cases of the former would be a waste of your time and mine, and certainly very boring. I will present some instances of the latter, and you can see that more thinking should have been done before these people spoke. You may question the title of the chapter. After you finish this section, you will wonder about the quotes.

In answer to the question about living forever, Eva Lasting, a Miss USA contestant replied,

"I would not live forever, because we should not live forever, because if we were supposed to live forever, then we would live forever, but we cannot live forever, which is why I would not live forever."

Married to her forever might be quite a challenge!

*****

"Whenever I watch TV and see those poor starving kids all over the world, I can't help but cry. I mean I would like to be

skinny like that, but not with all those flies and death and stuff."
- pop singer Dee Lited

*****

"Smoking kills. If you're killed, you've lost a very important part of your life." - actress Ima Bewildered, during an interview to become spokesperson for the federal anti-smoking campaign

I don't think she got the title.

*****

"I've never had major knee surgery on any other part of my body." - Crash deBoards, University of Kentucky basketball forward

What about minor surgery?

*****

"Outside of the killings, Washington has one of the lowest crime rates in the country." - Mayor Carrie N. Anyway

*****

"I'm not going to have some reporters pawing through our papers. We are the President." First Lady, Keepit Hidden, commenting on the release of subpoenaed documents

I didn't think kings and queens were part of a democracy.

*****

"I don't feel we did wrong in taking this great country away from them. There were great numbers of people who needed new

land, and the Indians were selfishly trying to keep it to themselves."
- actor Liev deLand

*****

"Half this game is ninety percent mental." - baseball manager
Nat Shunalpastime

When you're through managing, there's an opening in math at the local high school.

*****

"It isn't pollution that's harming the environment. It's the impurities in our air and water that are doing it." - Vice President Howie Cares

I hope he's not currently teaching earth science.

*****

"I love California. I practically grew up in Phoenix." - Vice President Ida Know

Did I miss some news about California annexing Arizona?

*****

"I know how hard it is for you to put food on your family."
- President Pas dePotatoes

And he wonders why his grocery bills are so high.

*****

"It's no exaggeration to say that the undecideds could go one way or the other." - politician Ima Notsure

Not if they don't vote at all.

*****

"We've got to pause and ask ourselves: How much clean air do we need?" - auto executive Justa Pollutin

In his case, it probably won't matter.

*****

"I was provided with additional input that was radically different from the truth. I assisted in furthering that version." - Colonel Mora Lyes, from his testimony

Guess who missed ethics class?

*****

"This is unparalyzed in the state's history." - House Speaker, N. Leslie Taxed

*****

"The word 'genius' isn't applicable in football. A genius is a guy like Norman Einstein." - Seymour Concussions, NFL quarterback turned sports analyst

I wasn't aware that Albert had a twin brother.

*****

"I will make sure that everyone who has a job wants a job."
- President Ivan Searching

*****

"We don't necessarily discriminate. We simply exclude certain types of people." - Colonel Will Brainwash, ROTC Instructor.

Who said "military intelligence" wasn't an oxymoron?

*****

"If we don't succeed, we run the risk of failure." - President Nat Shirlee

I just discovered a new use for duct tape.

*****

"I'm going to be coming out here with my own drug problem."
- President Amy T. Please

*****

"I think anybody who doesn't think I'm smart enough to handle the job is misunderestimating." - politician Buya DeVotes

*****

"We are ready for an unforeseen event that may or may not occur." - Vice President Ima Redundant

*****

"Traditionally, most of Australia's imports come from overseas." - Dawn Undir

That's not necessarily true. Some may have arrived from Jupiter!

*****

"I want to thank each and every one of you for having extinguished yourselves this session." - House Speaker, Needa Vote

*****

"Keep good relations with the Grecians." - President Mia Formula

*****

"I hope I stand for anti-bigotry, anti-Semitism, anti-racism. This is what drives me." - President Carrie deCountry

*****

"I cannot tell you how grateful I am——I am filled with humidity." - State Legislator N. Nonomous, thanking his colleagues for re-electing him

That's what he gets for staying out in the rain too long.

*****

"I've always liked John La Care, Le Carrier, or however you pronounce his name. I'm mainly a history person." - President Eubie Supportive, talking about his literary preferences

*****

The phrase, "He gave 110%," has been quoted by so many people, that I don't have space to mention them all here. Having been a math teacher and one who studied mathematics for an undergraduate degree, I can assure you that no one can achieve 110% in performance. The maximum is 100%, which is almost impossible to attain at that.

Despite this, people still feel you can achieve 103%. Let's look at a mathematical formula and see what we come up with. If

A, B, C, D, E, F, G, H, I, J, K, L, M, N, O, P, Q, R, S, T, U, V, W, X, Y, Z

is represented by

1, 2, 3, 4, 5, 6, 7, 8, 9, 10, 11, 12, 13, 14, 15, 16, 17, 18, 19, 20, 21, 22, 23, 24, 25, 26 respectively then

hard work is 8+1+18+4+23+15+18+11 or 98%.

Knowledge is 11+14+15+23+12+5+4+7+5 or 96%, but

attitude is 1+20+20+9+20+21+4+5 or 100%.

But, bull**** is 2+21+12+12+19+8+9+20 or 103%

and look how far ***kissing will get you.

***kissing is 1+19+19+11+9+19+19+9+14+7 or 127%.

If you are not sure what those two words with the asterisks represent, go back to the formula. With certainty we can conclude that hard work and knowledge will get you close to 100% while attitude will get you to the max, but bull**** and ***kissing will put you over the top.

*****

I close with a quote that will leave your head spinning. Read only if you dare!

"...there are known unknowns; there are things we know we know. There are known unknowns, that is to say there are things that we know we don't know. But there are also unknown unknowns. There are things we do not know we don't know." - White House Official Seymour Clarity

And you thought only dogs should be muzzled.

*****

3
PRODUCTS

I have a small butter tray in my refrigerator. When you turn it over, you will find the words, "Do Not Boil." Each evening I like to put a pot of water on the stove, bring it to a boil and then throw in the butter holder!

What were the people who produced this item thinking, or was there any intelligence involved on their part? As you will see, there is no limit to what words can be placed on an item or in the directions enclosed. Remember that a group of words put together may not make a sentence, nor may the combination make any sense. We have big business to thank for that. Without any more delay, here are products that are available today as well as some of the directions that I have run into. Some I can vouch for 100 percent, while the others I have only read about. Nevertheless, I would be willing to bet that most of these are indeed authentic.

On a bar of Dial soap, you can find the words, "Use like regular soap."

What if this is the first bar of soap that you ever encountered. Come on guys, can you be more specific?

*****

On some Swanson frozen dinners you will find: "Serving suggestion: Defrost."

What if you just got home and didn't have time to do that? Couldn't you just crunch on it until it melts in your mouth?

*****

Printed on the bottom of Tesco's Tiramisu dessert you can find the words, "Do not turn upside down."

I guess in this case, it's too late. Oh well, we'll know better next time, assuming we remember.

*****

"Product will be hot after heating," is printed on Marks & Spenser Bread Pudding.

That isn't true if we don't turn on the oven. There weren't any directions to do so on the packet.

*****

On packaging for a Rowenta iron, you will find, "Do not iron clothes on body."

But what if I'm in a hurry for a meeting and don't have time to remove my pants?

*****

"Do not drive a car or operate machinery after taking this medication," can be found on Boot's Children Cough Medicine.

Don't tell me I have to operate the forklift myself. I wanted the kids to do it.

*****

You can find these words on Nytol Sleep Aid, "Warning: May cause drowsiness."

I guess the backhoe work will have to wait until tomorrow.

*****

On many brands of Christmas lights you will see, "For indoor or outdoor use only."

My wife will be mad when she sees what I bought. She had other plans for the lights.

*****

Sainsbury's peanuts has the following, "Warning: contains nuts."

And you thought all the nuts wound up in the can.

*****

A local grocery store's flyer advertised, "No Nuts Golden Peanut Butter."

There's neither grapes nor nuts in Grape-Nuts, so maybe this ad is all right.

*****

I'm sure you've seen the sign in the supermarket trying to sell "all purpose shrimp." Does that mean that you can use the shrimp to clean dishes? This shrimp can play shortstop, catcher, pitcher or any other position on the field. It's very versatile.

*****

How about the separate controls in a car for temperature? This means a husband and wife can be in the same vehicle but each can experience a different climate. I hate to say this, but if they have to buy a car with this feature, I doubt that the marriage will last.

*****

You see all those commercials on the tube for SUVs. They can climb mountains, regardless of how high the snow is piled and they are advertised as off-the-road vehicles. But then, why do I see so many of them on the highways when I drive? I imagine people aren't really paying attention to the ads on television.

I also see Hummers and Humvees, so someone is buying them. Recently, I even saw a stretch Humvee. Do the automobile manufactures have to produce these behemoths? At this rate, it won't be long before people will be riding in tanks, cement trucks and steamrollers!

*****

If you fly American Airlines, you might find the following words on a packet of what else, nuts, "Instructions: Open packet, eat nuts."

Honey, what's the next step? Maybe I should summon the flight attendant.

*****

To go along with your peanuts, you may want a Pepsi or Coke. Why not get a stronger similar tasting drink with a Jolt? Apparently there wasn't enough caffeine in regular colas so a new fortified product came out. At least people won't fall asleep on the job.

*****

On a Swedish chainsaw could be found, "Do not attempt to stop chain with your hands or genitals."

No wonder I always wound up in the emergency room after cutting wood. Next time I'll read the directions.

*****

The instruction "Do not use while sleeping," can be found on a Sears' hairdryer.

I was wondering why my hair looked so disgusting after I awoke in the morning. All the time I thought my wife had something to do with it.

*****

To encourage shoplifters, you will see on a bag of Fritos, "You could be a winner! No purchase necessary. Details inside."

Whoever came up with this probably had the IQ of a Frito, but only one.

*****

On a Japanese food processor you will see, "Not to be used for the other use."

Somehow I think perversion is involved here.

*****

I never understood the intelligence behind the invention of the portable video recorder. A VCR was invented to record programs when you weren't at home. The obsession with television can only be to blame for this gizmo.

*****

"Wearing of this garment does not enable you to fly," can be found on a child's Superman costume.

If I put on a Moses' costume, will I be able to lead the people into the land of milk and money?

*****

Answering machines have been around for some time and they can be useful. They are used when you dial someone's phone and get no answer. The machine doesn't answer you either. So then why is it called an answering machine? Shouldn't it be called a "no answer machine," because when you leave a message that's exactly what you're going to get.

*****

While I am talking about that voice recorder, the height of lunacy has been attained with call waiting, call forwarding, caller ID, caller ID block and caller ID unblock. The next step will probably be caller ID re-block of the unblock.

*****

The inventor of gunpowder most likely wasn't thinking. I always felt he should be shot. What about all those "brilliant" scientists working on the atomic bomb? They may have been thinking about what they were working on, but probably not much else. The worse creations of all time have to do with gunpowder and bombs. Without them there would still be murder, but it would take a lot longer and people would be a great deal safer. Perhaps people should consider communication first rather than whip out their handguns!

*****

Whoever came up with those little tags that you find on fruit? Apparently they were created so the cashiers could identify what consumers were buying. However, I don't think that there is more than one type of red grape, green grape or plum inside the supermarket, so it seems to be redundant and certainly annoying to the customer. It can't be because the hired help can't tell the difference between a banana and a cherry, can it?

Here's my suggestion in this regard. Set up a bag of grapes or cherries and place one tag on each individual piece of fruit. Then follow the guy who came up with those tags and when he is not looking substitute the enhanced bag of fruit for the one in his grocery cart. If you have extra time, put two tags on each cherry or grape!

*****

Over half the people agree that one of the worst inventions of all time is the cell phone. At the very same time a greater percentage say they couldn't live without it. It's unusual, but citizens of the world thirty years ago survived without it.

*****

Finally, we come to toothpaste. I consider Polygrip to be the real toothpaste. When we uncap the tube, put some on our toothbrush, what are we trying to keep together (as in the word paste?) Perhaps the right word should be tooth cleanser, except it probably wouldn't sell. Anyway, if you look at some brands of toothpaste, you may still find these words, "For best results, roll up and squeeze as you go."

I can only assume that this admonition has something to do with my teeth and visits to the dentist. But if I follow this advice, I don't think it will reduce the number of cavities that I get. But if this is referring to the most advantageous way of emptying the tube, then it is incorrect again. The best way to do this is to put the tube in the path of a steamroller. A cement mixer may also do the trick. Just make sure you have your toothbrush handy.

*****

4
SIGNS AND WORDS

As a people, we need signs to help us out. It would be really challenging to travel across the country by automobile without any route or traffic signs. As you might guess, there are some out there on the road that one needs to question. But highway signs aren't the only types I will be getting into, and we won't need to look too far.

I'm sure all of you are very familiar with the sign, "Deer crossing—1/2 mile."

I knew deer were smart animals, but can they actually read this? Does the sign imply that they can only cross the road in this half mile interval? No, actually they can cross anywhere they want and any time they desire. If you get in their way I hope you have a big car with good insurance because these animals don't have collision coverage. Running into a deer on the road is no picnic but it could be worse. You could run into a moose!

*****

Not long ago I saw a sign on route 77 in Corfu that said, "Virtual height of bridge: 12 feet." Does this mean that there could be such a thing as "virtual clearance?" If so, would this be for "virtual trucks" and could I see them when they were approaching?

*****

A few years ago you couldn't drive too far without seeing the ubiquitous phrase in cars on windows and bumpers that said, "Baby on Board." I don't know about you but I think it is very cruel to put an infant on such a hard piece of wood. I'm sure a crib, car seat or small carrier would be so much more comfortable. And then parents wonder why babies cry so much. Get them off those boards! Those are intended for computer people. I'm sure you've seen the sign, "Programmer on board." For some of you, that will have to be explained.

*****

What about the sign on the highway that says, "Slow senior citizens?" They may not be fast but how will you feel when and if you get to be their age? Be careful or they'll beat you with their canes.

*****

I once saw a sign in a store that said, "Ears pierced while you wait." I was going to do a drop off in the morning on my way to work!

*****

I see these two words at many banks and when I log on to the web. They admonish you to stop in or click here for your "free gift." I thought all gifts were by their very nature "free." I want the gift that you have to spend money to obtain. After all, there is no such thing as a free ride. You pay for what you get.

Nonetheless, it is amazing what people will pursue and acquire if it's "free." They will accept an elephant if there is no cost to get it, even if they can't feed it, house it or figure out a place that will take it when they get bored with it. These "free gifts" are the reason why the landfills are full and we see all those yard and garage sales.

*****

There's a preponderance of pizza places in every town in this country. In Western New York, we have one such establishment with the name "Just Pizza." But don't worry; you can also buy other types of food there, such as Buffalo wings. Maybe they should change their name!

*****

There was a pizza joint in Woburn, Massachusetts some years ago that advertised free delivery. There was just one problem. They didn't have a phone in the establishment, or wouldn't give out the number. Thus you could drive to the place, place your order, drive home and the pizza would soon be delivered to your house. Somehow this whole procedure didn't seem quite right. Eventually the store closed.

*****

Recently I saw an ad in a supermarket flyer for "Hot rotisserie 3-legged chickens." They are probably from Chernobyl or Three Mile Island. I won't buy any of those fowl.

*****

Close to the interstate rest areas you might see, "Pet Exercise Area." Are they in training for something I don't know about?

*****

Speaking of the interstate, I was driving on that highway when I saw the sign, "No exit." Oh no, I'll never be able to get off!

*****

Not that long ago you could see a sign at a gas station that read, "Regular Unleaded Gas." This one is puzzling. Did that gas have lead in it?

*****

I'm sure you've seen the bumper sticker "Fight Pollution——Ride a Horse." It's a great thought, but putting this sign on a car seems to defeat the purpose. Any car owner with this on the bumper is not practicing what he preaches. He would be doing that if he left his car in the garage all the time, but then no one would see his bumper. The auto add-on would be fine on the back of a bicycle if you could find the room for it. However, the best place for this bumper sticker is on the back of a horse, if he'll let you put it there!

*****

Across the nation in many places you will see a sign that says, "Office Park." I beg your pardon, but if I go to the park, I don't want to be anywhere near an office!

*****

Bumper stickers convey a message in many instances. But there are times when you start to wonder about them. Consider the one that admonishes, "Schools in session——drive carefully." This certainly is a good warning to us all, but does it imply that from the end of June until Labor Day we should drive like maniacs, filled with road rage?

*****

I saw a sign on a Mercedes not long ago that said, "No radio in car." All along I thought a Mercedes Benz was a luxury car! I bet the people in the car are sweltering with no air conditioning and they're probably sitting on orange crates.

*****

Following this up, I saw a bumper sticker on an old rundown clunker, which advertised, "My Mercedes is in the shop." Obviously it is not there to get its radio fixed!

*****

I saw a cement truck with the sign on the back that said, "Do not push." I guess if it has problems with the battery, we can't get it going by pushing it and popping the clutch.

*****

Every so often you see license plates that you can't figure out. Of course, that's why they're called vanity plates. I just hope that the owner knows what they mean. Along the road you can find bewildering signs as well. One I saw admonished, "No passing over 8 feet wide." I haven't got a clue on that one. Another said, "Use both lanes." But my car isn't that wide. Another puzzling sign is "Free dog dip." For the life of me I cannot figure this one out. Perhaps it is just some kind of canine fondue. Maybe it is nothing more than a special at a far eastern restaurant!

*****

Not long ago I saw a sign on the interstate that read, "Urgent message when flashing." When I passed it, it was doing just that so I wondered how they knew I was there. I was trying to get away from all that.

*****

I bought a house some time ago and as expected, received some documents afterward. On one of them were the words, "Original Copy." How could it be original if it was a copy? I never did care much for banks.

*****

While picking up a copy of the paper one day, I saw a sign on the convenience store that said, "After dark, store has less than $30." There must be a cash pickup every half-hour each night or else the store is about to close. I don't think that sign will keep robbers away. Perhaps it should be replaced with one that says, "This store guarded by a 357 Magnum three days a week——you guess which days!"

*****

A while ago I saw the words, "Illiterate——write for help." Sad to say, I think the author of this was serious.

*****

Many times people write things without proofreading or using spell checker on their PC. This can make for some very amusing reading, especially if it happens to be the church bulletin. I didn't change these names!

Bertha Belch, a missionary from Africa, will be speaking tonight at Calvary Methodist. Come hear Bertha Belch all the way from Africa.

You may not want to sit in the first row for this.

*****

Announcement in a church bulletin for a national Prayer and Fasting Conference: "The cost for attending the Fasting & Prayer Conference includes meals."

Some people don't practice what they preach.

*****

The sermon this morning: "Jesus Walks on the Water." The sermon tonight: "Searching for Jesus."

Will the deep-sea divers be brought in?

*****

Our youth basketball team is back in action Wednesday at 8 p.m. in the recreation hall. Come out and watch us kill Christ the King.

I thought the game was against St. John the Baptist.

*****

"Ladies, don't forget the rummage sale. It's a chance to get rid of those things not worth keeping around the house. Don't forget your husbands."

For those of you single women, you can rummage for a mate.

*****

The peacemaking meeting scheduled for today has been canceled due to a conflict.

*****

Remember in prayer the many who are sick of our community. Smile at someone who is hard to love. Say "Hell" to someone who doesn't care much about you.

*****

Don't let worry kill you off——let the Church help.

*****

Miss Charlene Mason sang "I Will Not Pass This Way Again," giving obvious pleasure to the congregation.

It could have been worse. She could have sung, "I'll Be With You Always."

*****

For those of you who have children and don't know it, we have a nursery downstairs.

If they don't know it, I doubt that they'll pick the kids up afterwards.

*****

Next Thursday there will be tryouts for the choir. They need all the help they can get.

*****

Barbara remains in the hospital and needs blood donors for more transfusions. She is also having trouble sleeping and requests tapes of Pastor Jack's sermons.

*****

The Rector will preach his farewell message after which the choir will sing, "Break Forth Into Joy."

I would have preferred, "Alleluia."

*****

Irving Benson and Jessie Carter were married on October 24th in the church. So ends a friendship that began in their school days.

*****

At the evening service tonight, the sermon topic will be "What Is Hell?" Come early and listen to our choir practice.

You may want to bring some earplugs.

*****

Scouts are saving aluminum cans, bottles and other items to be recycled. Proceeds will be used to cripple children.

Will there be a fundraiser later to help these injured kids?

*****

A bean supper will be held on Tuesday evening in the church hall. Music will follow.

One of the songs you might hear is Mason Williams' "Classical Gas."

*****

Eight new choir robes are currently needed due to the addition of several new members and to the deterioration of some older ones.

Vocal chords are one of the first things to go!

*****

Please place your donation in the envelope along with the deceased person you want remembered.

I don't think there's enough room.

*****

Attend and you will hear an excellent speaker and heave a healthy lunch.

You may want to sit as far in the back as possible.

*****

The church will host an evening of fine dining, superb entertainment and gracious hostility.

I wonder if there's something in the food.

*****

Potluck supper Sunday at 5:00 p.m.——prayer and medication to follow.

It doesn't sound like the attendees will be that "lucky."

*****

The ladies of the Church have cast off clothing of every kind. They may be seen in the basement on Friday afternoon.

What did you expect? They're doing a production of "Hair."

*****

This evening at 7 p.m. there will be a hymn sing in the park across from the Church. Bring a blanket and come prepared to sin.

Who said this church wasn't fun?

*****

Ladies Bible Study will be held Thursday morning at 10 a.m. All ladies are invited to lunch in the Fellowship Hall after the B.S. is done.

*****

The pastor would appreciate it if the ladies of the congregation would lend him their electric girdles for the pancake breakfast next Sunday.

This must be a new fashion statement.

*****

Low Self-Esteem Support Group will meet Thursday at 7 p.m. Please use the back door.

*****

The eighth-graders will be presenting Shakespeare's Hamlet in the Church basement Friday at 7 p.m. The congregation is invited to attend this tragedy.

*****

Weight Watchers will meet at 7 p.m. at the First Presbyterian Church. Please use large double door at the side entrance.

It could have been worse. You could have been directed to use the garage door.

*****

The Associate Minister unveiled the church's new tithing campaign slogan last Sunday: "I upped my pledge——up yours."

*****

Our next song is: "Angels We Have Heard Get High."

*****

Since I am dealing with an aspect of life that transcends the normal, I close with a sign I saw recently at a Psychic Healing Center. It advertised its business and said "walk-ins welcome." On the very same sign it said, "call for an appointment." Aren't these two contradictory? On the other hand, if these people running the business are that good, wouldn't they know that I was on my way to the clinic?

*****

5
DISORDER IN THE COURT

There will be mention of some decisions handed down by judges in the chapter dealing with various awards. The following are actual statements made during court cases. As you will see, the absence of intelligence is not limited to plaintiffs or defendants alone.

Judge: I know you, don't I?
Defendant: Uh, yes.
Judge: All right, tell me, how do I know you?
Defendant: Judge, do I have to tell you?
Judge: Of course, you might be obstructing justice not to tell me.
Defendant: Okay. I was your bookie.

*****

From a defendant representing himself...
Defendant: Did you get a good look at me when I allegedly stole your purse?
Victim: Yes, I saw you clearly. You are the one who stole my purse.
Defendant: I should have shot you while I had the chance.

*****

Judge: The charge here is theft of frozen chickens. Are you the defendant?

Defendant: No, sir, I'm the guy who stole the chickens.

I wonder if he works for the Colonel.

*****

Lawyer: How do you feel about defense attorneys?

Juror: I think they should all be drowned at birth.

Lawyer: Well, then, you are obviously biased for the prosecution.

Juror: That's not true. I think prosecutors should be drowned at birth, too.

*****

Judge: Is there any reason you could not serve as a juror in this case?

Juror: I don't want to be away from my job that long.

Judge: Can't they do without you at work?

Juror: Yes, but I don't want them to know it.

*****

Lawyer: Tell us about the fight.

Witness: I didn't see no fight.

Lawyer: Well, tell us what you did see.

Witness: I went to a dance at the Turner house and as the men swung around and changed partners, they would slap each other and one fellow hit harder than the other one liked and so the other one hit back and somebody pulled a knife and a rifle that had been hidden under a bed and the air was filled with yelling and smoke and bullets.

Lawyer: You, too, were shot in the fracas?

Witness: No sir, I was shot midway between the fracas and the navel.

If the shot were higher up, it would have done less damage.

*****

Defendant: Judge, I want you to appoint me another lawyer.

Judge: And why is that?

Defendant: Because the Public Defender isn't interested in my case.

Judge (to Public Defender): Do you have a comment on the defendant's motion?

Public Defender: I'm sorry, your Honor. I wasn't listening.

*****

Judge: Please identify yourself for the record.

Defendant: Colonel Ebenezer Jackson.

Judge: What does the "Colonel" stand for?

Defendant: Well, it's kinda like the "Honorable" in front of your name—not a damn thing.

*****

Judge: You are charged with habitual drunkenness. Have you anything to say in your defense?

Defendant: Habitual thirstiness?

*****

Question: Are you sexually active?
Answer: No, I just lie there.

*****

Question: What gear were you in at the moment of impact?
Answer: Gucci sweats and Reeboks.

Is that between second and third gear?

*****

Defendant (after being sentenced to 90 days in jail): Can I address the court?

Judge: Of course.

Defendant: If I called you a son of a bitch, what would you do?

Judge: I'd hold you in contempt and assess an additional five days in jail.

Defendant: What if I thought you were a son of a bitch?

Judge: I can't do anything about that. There's no law against thinking.

Defendant: In that case, I think you're a son of a bitch.

*****

A New Orleans lawyer sought an FHA loan for a client. He was told the loan would be granted if he could prove satisfactory title to a parcel of property being offered as collateral. The title to the property dated back to 1803, which took the lawyer three months to track down. After sending the information to the FHA, he received the following reply:

"Upon review of your letter adjoining your client's loan application, we note that the request is supported by an Abstract of

Title. While we compliment the able manner in which you have prepared and presented the application, we must point out that you have only cleared title to the proposed collateral property back to 1803. Before final approval can be accorded, it will be necessary to clear the title back to its origin."

Annoyed, the lawyer responded as follows:

"Your letter regarding title in Case No. 189156 has been received. I note that you wish to have title extended further than the 194 years covered by the present application. I was unaware that any educated person in this country, particularly those working in the property area, would not know that Louisiana was purchased by the United States from France in 1803, the year of origin identified in our application.

"For the edification of uninformed FHA bureaucrats, the title to the land prior to U.S. ownership was obtained from France, which had acquired it by Right of Conquest from Spain. The land came into the possession of Spain by Right of Discovery made in the year 1492 by a sea captain named Christopher Columbus, who had been granted the privilege of seeking a new route to India by the Spanish monarch, Isabella. The good queen, Isabella, being a pious woman and almost as careful about titles as the FHA, took the precaution of securing the blessing of the Pope before she sold her jewels to finance Columbus' expedition.

"Now the Pope, as I'm sure you may know, is the emissary of Jesus Christ, the Son of God, and God, it is commonly accepted, created this world. Therefore, I believe it is safe to presume that God also made that part of the world called Louisiana. God, therefore, would be the owner of origin and His origins date back, to before the beginning of time, the world as we know it, and the FHA. I hope to hell you find God's original claim to be satisfactory.

"Now, may we have our damn loan?"

Yes, the loan was approved.

Now you know why it takes so long to close on a home.

*****

Question: What is your date of birth?
Answer: July 15th.
Question: What year?
Answer: Every year.

*****

Question: This myasthenia gravis, does it affect your memory at all?
Answer: Yes.
Question: And in what ways does it affect it?
Answer: I forget.
Question: You forget? Can you give me an example of something that you've forgotten?

*****

Question: How old is your son, the one living with you?
Answer: Thirty-eight or thirty-five, I can't remember which.
Question: How long has he lived with you?
Answer: Forty-five years.

*****

Question: What was the first thing your husband said to you when he woke that morning?
Answer: He said, "Where am I, Cathy."
Question: And why did that upset you?
Answer: My name is Susan.

*****

Question: Do you know if your daughter has ever been involved in voodoo or the occult?

Answer: We both do.

Question: Voodoo?

Answer: We do.

Question: You do?

Answer: Yes, voodoo.

I wonder if the names of the parties involved in this discussion are Bud and Lou.

*****

Question: Now doctor, isn't it true that when a person dies in his sleep, he doesn't know about it until the next morning?

Answer: Did you actually pass the bar exam?

*****

Question: The youngest son, the twenty-year old, how old is he?

*****

Question: Were you present when your picture was taken?

*****

Question: So the date of conception of the baby was August 8th?

Answer: Yes.

Question: And what were you doing at that time?

*****

Question: She had three children, right?
Answer: Yes.
Question: How many were boys?
Answer: None.
Question: Were there any girls?

*****

Question: How was your first marriage terminated?
Answer: By death.
Question: And by whose death was it terminated?

*****

Question: Can you describe the individual?
Answer: He was about medium height and had a beard.
Question: Was this a male or a female?

*****

Question: Is your appearance here this morning pursuant to a
deposition notice, which I sent to your attorney?
Answer: No, this is how I dress when I go to work.

*****

Question: Doctor, how many autopsies have you performed
on dead people?
Answer: All my autopsies are performed on dead people.

*****

Question: All your responses must be oral, OK? What school
did you go to?
Answer: Oral.

*****

Question: Are you qualified to give a urine sample?

*****

Question: Doctor, before you performed the autopsy, did you check for a pulse?

Answer: No.

Question: Did you check for blood pressure?

Answer: No.

Question: Did you check for breathing?

Answer: No.

Question: So, then it is possible that the patient was alive when you began the autopsy?

Answer: No.

Question: How can you be so sure, Doctor?

Answer: Because his brain was sitting on my desk in a jar.

Question: But could the patient have still been alive?

Answer: Yes, it is possible that he could have been alive and practicing law somewhere.

*****

Question: Do you recall the time that you examined the body?

Answer: The autopsy started around 8:30 p.m.

Question: And Mr. Dennington was dead at the time?

Answer: No, he was sitting at table wondering why I was doing an autopsy.

*****

6
GET YOUR AWARD

The Stella Award is in honor of Stella Liebeck, the 81-year-old lady who spilled coffee on herself and then sued McDonald's because it was too hot. She won the case and the Stella Award is named after her for the most frivolous lawsuit. Personally I think the award should have been named after the judge who let her win the case, or at least someone should have spilled hot coffee on him.

Another award that comes out every year in praise of stupidity is the Darwin Award. This is presented to several people each year, some no longer with us because of their "intelligence." Some of these situations are so disgusting and the ending so tragic that I will not list them here. I am only trying to entertain you, not disgust you. As I present each case, I will not distinguish one award from another, nor will I rank the performances in order of stupidity. Some of the recipients are not included here but rather in the chapter on Criminal Behavior. This is not to imply that some of the actions here aren't criminal!

The chef at a hotel in Switzerland lost a finger in a meat-cutting machine and, after a little hopping around, submitted a claim to his insurance company. The company, suspecting negligence, sent out one of its men to have a look for himself. He tried the machine out and lost a finger. The chef's claim was approved.

They should have sent at least one more individual for verification.

*****

A man who shoveled snow for an hour to clear a space for his car during a blizzard in Chicago returned with his vehicle to find a woman had taken the space. Understandably, he shot her.

This would never happen in Miami!

*****

After stopping for drinks at an illegal bar, a Zimbabwean bus driver found that the 20 mental patients he was supposed to be transporting from Harare to Beltway had escaped. Not wanting to admit his incompetence, the driver went to a nearby bus stop and offered everyone waiting there a free ride. He then delivered the passengers to the mental hospital, telling the staff that the patients were very excitable and prone to bizarre fantasies. The deception wasn't discovered for three days.

It would have taken longer than three days if the staff at the hospital were the passengers.

*****

An American teenager was in the hospital yesterday recovering from serious head wounds received from an oncoming train. When asked how he received the injuries, the lad told police that he was simply trying to see how close he could get his head to a moving train before he was hit.

Thank God he didn't try this with an 747.

*****

In January 2000, Carrie Awn of Austin, Texas was awarded $780,000 by a jury of her peers after breaking her ankle tripping over a toddler who was running inside a furniture store. The owners of the store were understandably surprised at the verdict, considering the misbehaving little brat was Ms. Awn's son.

They should have forced the jury to baby-sit the kid for an evening!

*****

In June of 1998, 19-year-old Dollar Missing of Los Angeles won $74,000 and medical expenses when his neighbor ran over his hand with a Honda Accord. Mr. Missing apparently didn't notice there was someone at the wheel of the car, when he was trying to steal his neighbor's hubcaps.

No one said being a thief was an easy job.

*****

In May 2000, A Philadelphia restaurant was ordered to pay Shirley U. Jest of Lancaster, Pennsylvania $113,500 after she slipped on a soft drink and broke her coccyx. The beverage was on the floor because Ms. Jest threw it at her boyfriend thirty seconds earlier during an argument.

If the restaurant had chained her to the seat, this would never have happened.

*****

In October 1999, Hi Calibre of Little Rock, Arkansas was awarded $14,500 and medical expenses after being bitten on the buttocks by his next-door neighbor's beagle. The beagle was on a chain in its owner's fenced-in yard. The award was less than sought because the jury felt the dog might have been just a little provoked at the time by Mr. Calibre who was shooting it repeatedly with a pellet gun.

The next time the neighbor will get a pit bull and not have to worry about any frivolous lawsuit.

*****

In December 1997, Leeva deScene of Claymont, Delaware successfully sued the owner of a nightclub in a neighboring city when she fell from the bathroom window to the floor and knocked out her two front teeth. This occurred while Ms. deScene was trying to sneak through the window in the ladies room to avoid paying the $3.50 cover charge. She was awarded $12,000 and dental expenses.

Bars on the windows would have prevented this.

*****

According to police in Dahlonega, Georgia, ROTC cadet Ima Patsy, 20, was stabbed to death by fellow cadet, Mark Myword, 23, who was trying to prove that a knife could penetrate the flak vest that Patsy was wearing.

*****

Eubie Missingbrains was hospitalized in Andover Township, New Jersey and his wife Clueless was also injured by a quarter stick of dynamite that blew up in their car. While driving around at 2 a.m., the bored couple lit the dynamite and tried to toss it out the window to see what would happen, but they apparently failed to notice that the window was closed.

They should have had a convertible!

*****

According to The Washington Post of June 6, 1996, Harry Numnutz, 19, and an alleged accomplice, were arrested in West Lafayette, Indiana the previous month on theft and fraud charges. Numnutz allegedly cashed checks that he had written with disappearing ink, apparently believing the checks would be blank by the time they were presented to the bank for collection. However, traces of ink remained and police said Numnutz would have had a better chance of getting away with his plan if he had not used preprinted checks with his name and account number on them.

He should have used stolen checks.

*****

In Elyria, Ohio, Homey B. Gone, attempting to clean out cobwebs in his basement, declined to use a broom in favor of a propane torch and caused a fire that burned the first and second floors of his house.

A smoke alarm probably wouldn't have helped. At least the cobwebs are gone!

*****

In Guthrie, Oklahoma, Shirley Nothandy tried to kill a millipede with a shot from her .22-caliber rifle, but the shot ricocheted off a rock near the hole and hit pal Vi Olated in the head, fracturing her skull.

*****

In November 2000, Mr. Hugo Away of Oklahoma City purchased a brand new 32-foot Winnebago motor home. On his first trip home, having joined the freeway, he set the cruise control at 70 mph and calmly left the drivers seat to go into the back and make himself a cup of coffee. Not surprisingly the Winnie left the freeway, crashed and overturned. Mr. Away sued Winnebago for not advising him in the handbook that he couldn't actually do this. He was awarded $1,750,000 plus a new Winnie. Winnebago actually changed their handbooks on the back of this court case, just in case there are any other complete morons buying their vehicles.

In this case, I don't think a warning in the handbook would have made any difference.

*****

7

MISSING MARBLES

From the previous chapters, you may think that the lack of smarts arose because some people thought that when God created them, he was offering "grains" not "brains." They refused since they are into the low carbohydrate agenda. But actually everyone has an intellect. Some people just don't take full advantage of it. Some years ago, people used to have a sign on their desks that said, "THINK." The IBM Corporation was responsible for this simple, important admonition that doesn't seem to have been followed too much. Here are some more instances to entertain you. These events were chronicled by others, not by me personally.

This week, all our office phones went dead and I had to contact the telephone repair people. They promised to be out between 8:00 a.m. and 7:00 p.m. When I asked if they could give me a smaller time window, the pleasant gentleman asked, "Would you like us to call you before we come?" I replied that I didn't see how he would be able to do that, since our phones weren't working. He also requested that we report future outages by email (Does your email work without a telephone line?)

Obviously, this incident took place before the preponderance of cell phones and DSL. There is something else here I'm sure you have experienced waiting for a hookup of cable or phone service. It's that time estimate. Isn't there enough intelligence at these places so that they could give you a smaller window?

*****

I was signing the receipt for my credit card purchase when the clerk noticed I had never signed my name on the back of the credit card. She informed me that she could not complete the transaction unless the card was signed. When I asked why, she explained that it was necessary to compare the signature I had just signed on the receipt. So I signed the credit card in front of her. She carefully compared the signature to the one I had just signed on the receipt. As luck would have it, they matched.

This clerk sounds like a good candidate for guarding our country. Recently, something very similar happened to me at the post office, but not quite as bewildering as this.

*****

The stoplight on the corner buzzes when it's safe to cross the street. I was crossing with an intellectually challenged co-worker of mine when she asked if I knew what the buzzer was for. I explained that it signals blind people when the light is red. Appalled, she responded, "What on earth are blind people doing driving?"

The seeing-eye dog was on vacation so he had no choice but to drive.

*****

I live in a semi-rural area. We recently had a new neighbor call the local township administrative office to request the removal of the deer crossing sign on our road. The reason: too many deer were being hit by cars and he didn't want them to cross there anymore.

It's good to see that someone is concerned about wildlife!

*****

My daughter went to a local Taco Bell and ordered a taco. She asked the person behind the counter for "minimal lettuce." He said he was sorry, but they only had iceberg.

Did you ever wonder what the IQ of a kiwi is?

*****

I was at the airport, checking in at the gate when an airport employee asked, "Has anyone put anything in your baggage without your knowledge?" To which I replied, "If it was without my knowledge, how would I know?" He smiled knowingly and nodded, "That's why we ask."

Now you know why some people working for the government don't deserve pay raises.

*****

At a good-bye luncheon for an old and dear co-worker who is leaving the company due to "downsizing," our manager commented cheerfully, "This is fun. We should do this more often." Not a word was spoken. We all just looked at each other with that deer-in-the-headlights stare.

There's no doubt: the wrong person got terminated.

*****

I work with an individual who plugged her power strip back into itself and for the life of her couldn't understand why her system would not turn on.

Did you ever try forwarding a phone call from your phone to another number, which then forwards it back to your phone? You'd be surprised how quiet the cubicle will become.

*****

A lady at work was seen putting a credit card into her floppy drive and pulling it out very quickly. When I inquired as to what she was doing, she said she was shopping on the Internet and they kept asking for a credit card number, so she was using the ATM 'thingy.'

I wonder what she would do for internet sex.

*****

When my husband and I arrived at an automobile dealership to pick up our car, we were told the keys had been locked in it. We went to the service department and found a mechanic working feverishly to unlock the driver's side door. As I watched from the passenger side, I instinctively tried the door handle and discovered that it was unlocked. "Hey," I announced to the technician, "It's open!" To which he replied, "I know——I already got that side."

Do you think this technician is dating the woman with the ATM "thingy?"

*****

Recently, when I went to McDonald's, I saw on the menu that you could have an order of 6, 9 or 12 Chicken McNuggets. I asked for a half dozen nuggets. "We don't have half-dozen nuggets," said the teenager at the counter. "You don't?" I replied. "We only have six, nine, or twelve," was the reply. "So I can't order a half dozen nuggets, but I can order six?" "That's right." So I shook my head and ordered six McNuggets.

This server won't have a chance if the store goes "metric."

*****

I was checking out at the local Wal-Mart with just a few items and the lady behind me put her things on the belt close to mine. I picked up one of those dividers that they keep by the cash register and placed it between our things so they wouldn't get mixed. After the girl had scanned all of my items, she picked up the "divider", looking it all over for the bar code so she could scan it. Not finding the bar code she said to me, "Do you know how much this is?" I said to her, "I've changed my mind; I don't think I'll buy that today." She said "OK" and I paid her for the things and left. She had no clue to what had just happened.

*****

I recently saw a distraught young lady weeping beside her car. "Do you need some help?" I asked. She replied, "I knew I should have replaced the battery to this remote door unlocker. Now I can't get into my car. Do you think they (pointing to a distant convenience store) would have a battery to fit this?" "Hmmm, I dunno. Do you have an alarm, too?" I asked. "No, just this remote thingy," she answered, handing it and the car keys to me. As I took the key and manually unlocked the door, I replied, "Why don't you drive over there and check about the batteries. It's a long walk."

*****

Several years ago, we had an intern who was none too swift. One day she was typing and turned to a secretary and said, "I'm almost out of typing paper. What do I do?" "Just use copier machine paper," the secretary told her. With that, the intern took her last remaining blank piece of paper, put it on the photocopier and proceeded to make five "blank" copies.

*****

My neighbor works in the operations department in the central office of a large bank. Employees in the field call him when they have problems with their computers. One night he got a call from a woman in one of the branch banks who had this question: "I've got smoke coming from the back of my terminal. Do you guys have a fire downtown?"

It was just a birthday party for one of the gals.

*****

A mother calls 911 very worried, asking the dispatcher if she needs to take her kid to the emergency room; the kid was eating ants. The dispatcher tells her to give the kid some Benadryl and he should be fine, the mother says, "I just gave him some ant killer." The dispatcher then says, "Rush him in to emergency!"

Can you imagine being the teacher in a class with all these "mental giants?"

*****

AT&T fired President John Walter after nine months, saying he lacked intellectual leadership. He received a twenty-six million dollar severance package.

I doubt that Walter's the one who's lacking intelligence.

*****

A man spoke frantically into the phone, "My wife is pregnant and her contractions are only two minutes apart!" "Is this her first child?" the doctor asked? "No," the man shouted, "This is her husband!"

Remember, she was the one who married him!

*****

Lake Isabella is located in the high desert, an hour east of Bakersfield, California. This was the scene one summer for some boating novices, who were having problems. No matter how hard they tried, they couldn't get their brand new twenty-two foot going properly. It was very sluggish in almost every maneuver, no matter how much power was applied. After about an hour of trying to make it go, they putted to a nearby marina, thinking someone there could tell them what was wrong. A thorough topside check revealed everything in perfect working condition. The engine ran fine, the outdrive went up and down, the prop was the correct size and pitch. So, one of the marina guys jumped into the water to check underneath, he came up choking on water, because he was laughing so hard. Under the boat, still strapped securely in place, was the trailer.

They just wanted to save time hitching the boat later on their departure.

*****

8
Random Stupidity

I'm sure you've heard the expression, "People wondered if he lacked intelligence but then he spoke and removed all doubt." Personally, I think individuals who talk and talk and don't say anything shouldn't be allowed to speak. Of course, that thinking would keep many lawyers and politicians quiet. I guess that is a very good suggestion!

As you can tell from the title of the chapter, this will cover a myriad of instances where people weren't at their very best intellectually. I wouldn't be a bit surprised if there wasn't a connection between being a couch potato and some of these situations.

Ernie Pyle was a great reporter covering World War II who never made it back home. He was one of many journalists killed in action. Today, people in the media still travel to hostile areas to cover conflicts and I give them credit for their courage. Nonetheless, what were these individuals thinking when they decided to head overseas? Better yet, what was going through their minds when they arrived in Vietnam, Iraq or Afghanistan?

Every war is dangerous to soldiers, journalists and civilians alike, and they get more dangerous with each new confrontation because of the capabilities of the weapons. Since war brings with it the cessation of truth, it seems that just about any effort by a reporter will be a futile one, thanks to government sanctions of the coverage. Perhaps it is time to end wars and instead send journalists to areas of peace.

*****

The following story appeared in the Buffalo News on November 4, 2001.

In Mount Vision, New York, three teenagers have been charged with second-degree assault after shooting one another in the leg in what they considered "a test of courage," according to the police. The teens were arrested after they sought treatment from the school nurse for wounds on the calves of their legs, which were inflicted by a .22 caliber rifle.

Note that sane people did not say this was a "test of courage," only the teenagers involved. Maybe the correct phrase is "test of stupidity." Another observation is that this occurred in a place called Mount Vision, and it appeared that the perpetrators didn't have any, vision that is.

*****

Not too long ago I received a call on my answering machine that asked me to return the call. The person said that he would be up for another hour or so, but the caller did not specify what time it was. Granted, some answering machines have a time stamp for each call but mine doesn't and I'm sure the caller knew that. Needless to say I didn't return the call that night. Maybe I should have and asked him what time he called so I would know if I shouldn't have called when I did.

*****

From *Live By The Sword: The Secret War Against Castro And The Death Of JFK* by Gus Russo comes the following:

There was also a plan to spread the word on Cuba that the Second Coming of Christ was imminent, and that he would vanquish the anti-Christ Castro. A submarine would then surface near the island and send up starshells——supposedly a manifestation of the Second Coming, which would lead to Castro's overthrow. Assistant CIA Director Walt Elder called this plan "elimination by illumination."

I wonder if this was before or after they tried the exploding cigars.

*****

Thomas Friedman's book *From Beirut to Jerusalem* is an insightful narrative about the Middle East. War has always been lunacy and that will never change. You may want to read the entire book. These excerpts can be found in his book.

"One day we were throwing stones at soldiers all morning and they were charging at us. We were going back and forth," said Abu Laila from Kalandia. "Finally we sent one of ours up to one of theirs and said, 'You go eat and we'll go eat and we'll all come back later.' They agreed. So we all went home."

Actually, Beirut's wealthiest flocked to Goodies to buy all their food. A gaggle of Mercedes-Benzes could always be found parked outside. Legend had it that one day a disheveled young man entered Goodies, walked up to the cash register with a rifle, and demanded all the money. Within three seconds three different women drew their pistols out of their Gucci handbags, pumped a flurry of bullets into the thief, and then continued pushing their shopping carts down the bountiful aisles.

Two friends of mine hopped into a cab in West Beirut and headed to cover a big story in the Druse village of Hammama. The driver sped through the Druse checkpoint and soon the car was being pursued by these guys with big beards and guns poking out the windows. Soon they were surrounded, their pursuers were mad, shouting and shaking their fists and sticking their guns into the taxi.

The journalists were scared so they repeated the Arabic word for journalist and showed the aggressors their press credentials. The Druse militiamen examined them and eventually one asked, "Which of you is from Dallas?" One replied that he was and with that one of the gunmen pointed the gun into the car towards him and then asked, "Who shot JR?" Shortly after the Druse gunmen erupted into laughter and said, "Welcome to our town!"

*****

The following story was in the Buffalo News thanks to the Chicago Tribune.

A Chicago woman who stole nearly $250,000 from her employer to finance a shopping addiction has been spared from prison in a novel ruling by a federal judge who found that she bought expensive clothing and jewelry to "self-medicate" her depression. Elizabeth Roach racked up credit card bills of almost $500,000, buying a $9000 purse, a belt buckle for $7000 and hundreds of designer outfits. U.S. District Judge Matthew Kennelly ruled that Roach suffered from "a diminished mental capacity" that contributed to the commission of the crime.

They should give her a job shopping for the government.

*****

Not long ago, some Boeing employees on the airfield decided to steal a life raft from one of the 747s. They were successful in getting it out of the plane and home. Shortly after they took it for a float on the river, they noticed a Coast Guard helicopter coming towards them. It turned out that the chopper was homing in on the emergency locator beacon that activated when the raft was inflated. These individuals are no longer employed at Boeing.

*****

Having been a computer consultant, I was fortunate to have to read various technological manuals by IBM. I'm not sure if they came up with the following phrase, but I know they used it in their publications. Others have used it as well. The expression is, "This page intentionally left blank." My question is, if the page is blank, why is there writing on it? It appears that it really isn't since I can't use it to print a letter. Those individuals who came up with this expression didn't exactly follow the IBM admonition to "THINK."

*****

To conclude the chapter, I usually don't watch much television, and certainly not the "reality shows." I was staying at a friend's house and he had on Ripley's Believe It Or Not. I was reading a book at the time but I couldn't help overhearing the program.

The first case had to do with an individual who in his spare time liked to literally "hang out." His method of doing this involved meat hooks placed into his skin. Thank God, I had my book and didn't have to view the proceedings. What some people won't do for "fame and glory" or for getting into a book of records.

The second person may have been stranger. He had this outrageous getup to protect and insulate himself and he looked like someone from another planet. He needed this outfit because 1,000,000 volts of electricity were going to be jolted through his body. He probably could have saved a great deal of money by using lightning instead of his contraption. The last I heard, he was still alive!

Fortunately the last person featured on the program was an artist. He created works that came from the inside——of his body. He didn't use paint, but rather excretions, such as regurgitations and anything else he could come up with from within.

Who said there isn't anything worthwhile on the tube? You may want to watch this program to get some ideas.

*****

9
OBSERVATIONS

Some time ago I went to the YMCA for some exercise. There was an individual there who was running laps, quite a few of them. After a while I heard him talking to a friend saying that he needed to run some miles since he was going to be drinking a lot of beer that evening. Certainly, running is better than sitting home watching the tube, but it can lead to leg injuries. Drinking all those brews isn't that healthy either. He would have been better off working out on the track for a short while and then have just one or two brewskis. What was he thinking?

Once a month we see the appearance of a full moon. At that time, people notice strange occurrences and behavior on the part of humans. It's blamed on that heavenly body. And yet why do we witness unusual events and actions by people during the middle of the day as well as when the moon is only in the first quarter? It looks like the blame is in the wrong place.

People do all kinds of weird things. We have extreme sports, people almost flying down mountains on skis or boards, individuals trying to scale vertical cliffs of ice, and others in Nepal trying to reach the top of Mt. Everest. Somehow these practices have made it to television in the form of reality shows. The worst part of that "improvement" of TV is that almost everyone tunes in to this schlock. If not, then why are these programs still being broadcast?

I don't even have to talk about any of the above but rather look at life in these United States for some interesting phenomena. Unfortunately, it may get worse with the passage of time.

Only in America can a pizza get to your home faster than an ambulance.

Maybe the hospitals should hire drivers from Domino's Pizza!

*****

Is there any other country besides ours that has handicapped parking in front of a skating rink?

This may be a weak argument since you have to applaud any challenged person who puts on a pair of skates. We do have the Special Olympics.

*****

In the United States, drugstores make the sick walk all the way to the back of the store to get their prescriptions while healthy people can buy cigarettes at the front.

Marketing people aren't that dumb!

*****

We travel to Burger King and McDonald's and order cheeseburgers, large fries and a diet coke.

We can't have all those calories from the regular coke.

*****

Where else do you see banks leave both doors open and then chain the pens to counters?

Those writing instruments cost a lot to replace. I'll bet they get them from the government. From some employees I have talked to at various banks, maybe they should be chained to a counter.

*****

Only in America do homeowners leave cars worth thousands of dollars in the driveway and put useless junk in the garage.

It's done so others won't catch a glimpse of their garbage.

*****

A person I worked with had call waiting on his phone so he wouldn't miss any calls from people he didn't want to talk to in the first place. Nevertheless, he didn't have an answering machine.

The machine must cost more than the call-waiting feature.

*****

"Politics" is the phrase we use in this country to describe the process so well. In Latin, "poli" means "many" and "tics" is another name for bloodsucking creatures.

That word fits perfectly.

*****

In the United States and probably Canada too, we can buy hot dogs in packages of ten and the rolls to hold them in packages of eight.

This may have something to do with an exchange rate.

*****

10
YOUNG INTELLIGENCE

Children are attending school and learning, so we can excuse them for some of the things they say. Fortunately, because of their youth, they utter "knowledge" that can be rather funny. There's no reason why I should leave out some of these gems.

A kindergarten teacher was observing her classroom of children while they drew. She would occasionally walk around to see each child's work. As she got to one little girl who was working diligently, she asked what the drawing was? The girl replied, "I'm drawing God." The teacher paused and said, "But no one knows what God looks like." Without missing a beat, or looking up from her drawing, the girl replied, "They will in a minute."

*****

A Sunday school teacher was discussing the Ten Commandments with her five and six-year-olds. After explaining the commandment to "Honor thy father and mother," she asked, "Is there a commandment that teaches us how to treat our brothers and sisters?" Without missing a beat one little boy (the oldest of a family) answered, "Thou shall not kill."

*****

An honest seven-year-old admitted calmly to her parents that Billy Brown had kissed her after class. "How did that happen?" gasped her mother. "It wasn't easy," admitted the young lady, "but three girls helped me catch him."

*****

One day a little girl was sitting and watching her mother do the dishes at the kitchen sink. She suddenly noticed that her mother had several strands of white hair sticking out in contrast on her brunette head. She looked at her mother and inquisitively asked, "Why are some of your hairs white, Mom?" Her mother replied, "Well, every time that you do something wrong and make me cry or unhappy, one of my hairs turns white." The little girl thought about this revelation for while and then said, "Momma, how come all of grandma's hairs are white?"

*****

A three-year-old went with his dad to see a litter of kittens. On returning home, he breathlessly informed his mother that there were two boy kittens and two girl kittens. "How did you know?" his mother asked. "Daddy picked them up and looked underneath," he replied. "I think it's printed on the bottom."

*****

The children had all been photographed, and the teacher was trying to persuade them each to buy a copy of the group picture. "Just think how nice it will be to look at it when you are all grownup and say, 'There's Jennifer; she's a lawyer,' or 'That's Michael. He's a doctor.'" A small voice at the back of the room rang out, "And there's the teacher. She's dead."

*****

A teacher was giving a lesson on the circulation of the blood. Trying to make the matter clearer, she said, "Now, class, if I stood on my head, the blood, as you know, would run into it, and I would turn red in the face." "Yes," the class said. "Then why is it that while I am standing upright in the ordinary position the blood doesn't run into my feet?" A little fellow shouted, "'Cause yer feet ain't empty."

*****

Question: Name the four seasons.
Answer: Salt, pepper, mustard and vinegar.

*****

Question: Explain one of the processes by which water can be made safe to drink.
Answer: Flirtation makes water safe to drink because it removes large pollutants like grit, sand, dead sheep and canoeists.

*****

Question: How is dew formed?
Answer: The sun shines down on the leaves and makes them perspire.

*****

Question: How can you delay milk from turning sour?
Answer: Keep it in the cow.

*****

Question: What causes the tides in the oceans?
Answer: The tides are a fight between the earth and the moon. All water tends to flow toward the moon because there is no water on the moon and nature hates a vacuum. I forget where the sun joins in this fight.

*****

Question: What are steroids?
Answer: Things for keeping carpets still on the stairs.

*****

Question: What happens to your body as you age?
Answer: When you get old, so do your bowels and you get intercontinental.

*****

Question: What happens to a boy when he reaches puberty?
Answer: He says good-bye to his boyhood and looks forward to his adultery.

*****

Question: Name a major disease associated with cigarettes.
Answer: Premature death.

*****

Question: What is artificial insemination?
Answer: When the farmer does it to the cow instead of the bull.

*****

Question: How are the main parts of the body categorized (e.g., abdomen)?

Answer: The body is consisted into three parts——the brainium, the borax and the abdominal cavity. The brainium contains the brain; the borax contains the heart and lungs, and the abdominal cavity contains the five bowels, A, E, I, O and U.

The other letters of the alphabet must be "incontinence."

*****

Question: What is the fibula?
Answer: A small lie.

*****

Question: What does "varicose" mean?
Answer: Nearby.

*****

Question: Give the meaning of the term "Caesarean Section."
Answer: The Caesarean Section is a district in Rome.

And I thought that it was a group of people cheering at a soccer match in Italy.

*****

Question: What does the word "benign" mean?
Answer: Benign is what you will be after you be eight.

*****

I conclude the chapter with statements about the Bible and letters to God written by Sunday school students.

When the three wise guys from the East Side arrived, they found Jesus in the manger. He was born because Mary had an emaculate contraption. St. John the Blacksmith dumped water on Jesus' head.

*****

Jesus enunciated the Golden Rule, which says to do one to others before they do one to you.

*****

It was a miracle when Jesus rose from the dead and managed to get the tombstone off the entrance.

*****

The people who followed the Lord were called the twelve decibels.

*****

A Christian should have one wife. This is called monotony.

*****

The epistles were the wives of the apostles.

*****

One of the opossums was St. Matthew, who was by profession a taximan.

*****

When Mary heard she was the Mother of Jesus, she sang the Magna Carta.

*****

St. Paul cavorted to Christianity. He preached holy acrimony, which is another name for marriage.

*****

In the first book of the Bible, Guinessis, the Lord got tired of creating the world, so he took the Sabbath off.

*****

Adam and Eve were created from an apple tree.

*****

Noah's wife was called Joan of Arc. When Noah built the ark, the animals came on in pears.

*****

Lot's wife was a pillar of salt by day, but a ball of fire by night.

*****

The Jews were a proud people and throughout history they had trouble with unsympathetic Genitals.

*****

Sampson was a strongman who let himself be led astray by a jezebel like Delilah. He slated the Philistines with the axe of apostles.

*****

Moses led the Hebrews to the Red Sea, where they made unleavened bread, which is bread without any ingredients. He went up Mount Cyanide to get the Ten Amendments. He died before he ever reached the UK. Then Joshua led the Hebrews in the Battle of Geritol.

*****

The first commandment was when Eve told Adam to eat the apple. The fifth is humor thy mother and father. The seventh is thou shall not admit adultery.

*****

The greatest miracle in the Bible is when Joshua told his son to stand still and he obeyed him.

*****

David was a Hebrew king skilled at playing the liar. He fought with the Finkelsteins, a race of people who lived in biblical times.

*****

Solomon, one of David's sons, had 300 wives and 700 porcupines.

*****

Dear God,

Thank you for the baby brother but what I asked for was a puppy. I never asked for anything before. You can look it up. - Joyce

* * * * *

Dear Mr. God,

I wish you would not make it so easy for people to come apart. I had to have three stitches and a shot. - Janet

* * * * *

Dear God,

I read the Bible. What does beget mean? Nobody will tell me. Love, Alison

* * * * *

Dear God,

Is it true my father won't get into Heaven if he uses his golf words in the house? - Anita

* * * * *

Dear God,

My Grandpa says you were around when he was a little boy. How far back do you go? Love, Dennis

* * * * *

Dear God,

It is great the way you always get the stars in the right place. Why can't you do that with the moon? - Jeff

* * * * *

Dear God,
Please send Dennis Clark to a different summer camp this
year. - Peter

* * * * *

Dear God,
Maybe Cain and Abel would not kill each other so much if
they each had their own rooms. It works out OK with me and my
brother. - Larry

* * * * *

Dear God,
Is Reverend Coe a friend of yours, or do you just know him
through the business? - Donny

* * * * *

11
CRIMINAL BEHAVIOR

They say that crime doesn't pay. When you finish this chapter, you should be one hundred percent convinced of that. Whatever happened to competent crooks? Willie "The Actor" Sutton was in that class. You can read his story in the book *Where The Money Was*. Anyone who can do the deed and write about it is to be admired. From some of the following cases, most of these derelicts will be lucky if they can sign their own name.

This story originates in San Francisco. A man, wanting to rob a downtown Bank of America, walked into the branch and wrote "This iz a stikkup. Put all your muny in this bag" While standing in line, waiting to give his note to the teller, he began to worry that someone had seen him write the note and might call the police before he reached the teller's window. So he left the Bank of America and crossed the street to Wells Fargo. After waiting a few minutes in line, he handed his note to the Wells Fargo teller.

She read it and, surmising from his spelling errors that he wasn't the brightest light in the harbor, told him that she could not accept his stickup note because it was written on a Bank of America deposit slip and that he would either have to fill out a Wells Fargo deposit slip or go back to Bank of America. Looking somewhat defeated, the man said, "OK" and left. He was arrested a few minutes later, as he was waiting in line back at Bank of America.

Willie's not the only one turning over in his grave! It gets worse.

*****

A burglar in New Jersey stuck a piece of paper in the lock at an office building so he could sneak in later and rob it. The suspect was tracked down after police found the piece of paper. It was a parking ticket with the man's name and address on it.

I'll bet he wasn't going to pay the parking ticket!

*****

Two burglars from Sioux Falls, South Dakota broke into a local business but had trouble fitting the loot into their getaway car. The pair was nabbed after police saw a safe sticking out the back of their Honda Prelude.

Maybe that's why "vans" are used by "vandals."

*****

Two Argentine men were arrested after they tried to escape on a motor scooter with a stolen toilet. The pair had gone to a fast food restaurant in Buenos Aires and asked to use the bathroom. Then they yanked the toilet out and ran off with it. The police said it was "unclear" why the men wanted the toilet.

Anyone with the least bit of intelligence can see that they ate too many burritos!

*****

Police in Wichita, Kansas arrested a 22-year-old man at an airport hotel after he tried to pass two $16 bills.

He was probably giving change for a $35 bill.

*****

In Virginia, a bank robber was nabbed because he made the classic mistake of returning to the scene of the crime. He was collared after he tried to deposit some of the loot into the same bank he had robbed a month earlier. He was recognized because the same teller waited on him both times.

Wearing a mask at the time of the holdup or when he made the deposit might have been a good idea!

*****

Two armed men who had planned to rob a bank in Elkhart, Indiana were foiled when they discovered the branch only offered drive-through service. A passer-by told police that two men, wearing ski masks and carrying rifles, were loitering outside a Bank One branch but couldn't get inside. The men left before the police arrived.

If they had brought their car, they could have used the drive up window.

*****

A Gowanda, New York man who called police to report his car stolen left his stash of marijuana on the kitchen table when officers arrived to interview him. He was issued an appearance ticket by the investigator.

I'm sure he was inhaling.

*****

In Peoria, Arizona a man stood in line at a convenience store to buy some gum. The guy behind him was a cop who could smell the marijuana on him. The policeman asked, "Do you have any more dope?" The reply was, "No, we smoked it all earlier." He was soon arrested.

He didn't buy the gum soon enough.

*****

In Utica, New York, a thief broke into a car dealership. A policeman responded to the call and saw the light inside so he went closer and each stared at each other. The crook headed for the exit and so did the officer. They looked at each other again. The burglar then went to another exit with the same result. Finally the burglar surrendered saying, "I give up; the place is surrounded."

Why are there no degree programs for criminals?

*****

A man walked into a Louisiana Circle-K, put a twenty-dollar bill on the counter, and asked for change. When the clerk opened the cash drawer, the man pulled a gun and asked for all the cash in the register, which the clerk promptly provided. The man took the cash from the clerk and fled, leaving the twenty on the counter. The total amount of cash he got from the drawer—fifteen dollars.

If someone points a gun at you and gives you money, was a crime committed?

*****

In Fort Lauderdale, a bank robber handed the clerk a note but was told she didn't have that much cash and it might take a few minutes so he walked to the back of the line. Fifteen minutes passed and by this time the cops were on their way. The robber asked if the clerk was ready and he got the cash and was greeted by the police. The holdup note was written on the back of a job application he had filled out.

I didn't think thieves had to fill out applications for those jobs.

*****

A cat burglar entered a grocery store in Vermilion, Ohio from the roof. He fell through the ceiling and not far from a night crew stocking shelves. Shortly thereafter, he was arrested by the police. It turns out the store was open twenty-four hours a day!

I doubt that his brain worked more than a few hours each day. He probably should have been following his true profession—robbing cats!

*****

As a female shopper exited a New York convenience store, a man grabbed her purse and ran. The clerk called 911 immediately, and the woman was able to give them a detailed description of the snatcher. Within minutes, the police apprehended the snatcher. They put him in the car and drove back to the store. The thief was then taken out of the car and told to stand there for a positive ID. To which he replied, "Yes, officer, that's her. That's the lady I stole the purse from."

Some people really give the profession a bad name.

*****

A pair of Michigan robbers entered a record shop nervously waving revolvers. The first one shouted, "Nobody move!" When his partner moved, the startled first bandit shot him.

*****

In Milwaukee, Wisconsin a man entered a Taco Bell and announced, "This is a hold-up." Soon a reply came, "No, it's not," and he faced twenty-three weapons drawn. The Police Academy had just taken a lunch break there.

It would have still been risky, but he may have been luckier at a donut shoppe.

*****

In Oregon two bank robbers used dynamite to open a safe. They had inside information that it contained cash and they selected the time for the robbery based on the payroll period. They wound up buried in debris, brick, wood and dirt after the explosion and eventually in the hospital and prison. It turns out the company who inhabited the building left the safe and the new owners used it to store dynamite.

Apparently they didn't get enough inside information!

*****

Another robber encountered difficulties because of a video camera installed on the premises. He saw it and taped it so he could commit the crime. Unfortunately, he was apprehended because the video got his face before he did the tape job.

He should have used the duct tape on his face.

*****

An attempted robbery went awry because of the lookout. It seems he was almost legally blind. He could see shapes and as the robbery was taking place, someone came out and he thought it was his partner. He started talking to him about the break-in and was soon arrested.

They probably should have had a different lookout and used the blind guy at the actual holdup.

*****

In Laramie, Wyoming two men in a pickup truck ran out of gas and stopped for help at a police station. That wasn't a bad idea except the truck was stolen. They were soon behind bars. The truck did have two gas tanks, one of which was full but they didn't know about it.

Did they think they could get gas from the cops?

*****

Seems this Arkansas guy wanted some beer pretty badly. He decided that he'd just throw a cinderblock through a liquor store window, grab some booze, and run. So he lifted the cinderblock and heaved it over his head at the window. The cinderblock bounced back and hit the would-be thief on the head, knocking him unconscious. The liquor store window was made of Plexiglas. The whole event was caught on videotape.

He should have gotten some dynamite from the other robbers.

*****

A thief burst into a Florida bank one day wearing a ski mask and carrying a gun. Aiming his gun at the guard, the thief yelled, "Freeze, mother-stickers, this is a &#@%-UP!" For a moment, everyone was silent. Then the snickers started. The guard completely lost it and doubled over laughing. It probably saved his life, because he'd been about to draw his gun. He couldn't have drawn and fired before the thief got him. The thief ran away and is still at large.

In memory of the event, the bank later put a plaque on the wall engraved with the words, "Freeze, mother-stickers, this is a &#@%-UP!"

What exactly is a "mother-sticker?"

*****

The Ann Arbor News crime column reported that a man walked into a Burger King in Ypsilanti, Michigan, at 5 a.m., flashed a gun, and demanded cash. The clerk turned him down because he said he couldn't open the cash register without a food order. When the man ordered onion rings, the clerk said they weren't available for breakfast. Frustrated, the man walked away.

*****

A former employee of a fast food store tried to rob the very same store where he was employed. He had a gun and asked for money and a chalupa. Waiting for his food gave the police a chance to arrive. He never did get away—he tried to accomplish this on a bicycle.

The moral here is to never commit a robbery on an empty stomach!

*****

In Kentucky, two men tried to pull the front off a cash machine by running a chain from the machine to the bumper of their pickup truck. Instead of pulling the front panel off the machine, though, they pulled the bumper off their truck. Scared, they left the scene and drove home, without their bumper. Their vehicle's license plate was still attached to the bumper. They were quickly arrested.

Ever wonder what the IQ of a turnip is?

*****

When his 38-caliber revolver failed to fire at his intended victim during a holdup in Long Beach, California, would be robber Eubie Dum did something that can only inspire wonder: He peered down the barrel and tried the trigger again. This time it worked.

In this case the five-day waiting period for firearms wouldn't have made a difference.

*****

Police in Radnor, Pa., interrogated a suspect by placing a metal colander on his head and connecting it with wires to a photocopy machine. The message "He's lying" was placed in the copier, and police pressed the copy button each time they thought the suspect wasn't telling the truth. Believing the "lie detector" was working, the suspect confessed.

Why spend vast sums of money for police enforcement? You don't need it!

*****

Police in Oakland, California spent two hours attempting to subdue a gunman, who had barricaded himself inside his home.

After firing ten tear gas canisters, officers discovered that the man was standing beside them in the police line, shouting, "Please come out and give yourself up."

*****

In Modesto, California, Perry Clever was arrested for trying to hold up a Bank of America branch without a weapon. King used a thumb and a finger to simulate a gun, but unfortunately, he failed to keep his hand in his pocket.

At least he didn't have to go through the background check for the gun.

*****

An Illinois man, pretending to have a gun, kidnapped a motorist and forced him to drive to two different automated teller machines, where the kidnapper proceeded to withdraw money from his own bank accounts.

His car was in the shop and he just needed a ride.

* * * *

A man walked into a Topeka, Kansas Quick Stop, and asked for all the money in the cash drawer. Apparently, the take was too small, so he tied up the store clerk and worked the counter himself for three hours until police showed up and grabbed him.

There's nothing wrong with pitching in to help others.

*****

Police in Los Angeles had good luck with a robbery suspect who just couldn't control himself during a lineup. When detectives asked each man in the lineup to repeat the words, "Give me all your money or I'll shoot," the man shouted, "that's not what I said!"

It's important to be accurate.

*****

A guy walked into a little corner store with a shotgun and demanded all of the cash from the cash drawer. After the cashier put the cash in a bag, the robber saw a bottle of scotch that he wanted behind the counter on the shelf. He told the cashier to put it in the bag as well, but the cashier refused and said, "Because I don't believe you are over twenty-one." The robber said he was, but the clerk still refused to give it to him because he didn't believe him. At this point, the robber took his driver's license out of his wallet and gave it to the clerk. The clerk looked it over and agreed that the man was in fact over twenty-one and he put the scotch in the bag. The robber then ran from the store with his loot. The cashier promptly called the police and gave the name and address of the robber that he got off the license. They arrested the robber two hours later.

*****

I. M. Lonely broke into a home in Martinsburg, West Virginia on New Year's Eve, robbed the husband and wife of $540 and held them hostage for over an hour. He noticed a piano in the home and directed the husband to play. Lonely joined in by singing. Before long, he thought they should order some pizza and he began playing with his gun. The incident ended with Lonely's arrest after an event that happens time and again——he accidentally shot himself.

*****

In Cincinnati, Erne Yurpay pleaded guilty to robbery, which he wound up doing alone because his brother Istole refused to get involved because he felt Erne was too dumb. Erne was arrested after he accidentally hit himself over the head with a crowbar, leaving blood on the scene, which the authorities used to solve the crime.

It's fortunate he didn't have a chainsaw.

* * * * *

And last but not least, in October 1998 Stuck N. Side of Bristol, Pennsylvania was leaving a house he had just finished robbing by way of the garage. He was not able to get the garage door to go up since the automatic door opener was malfunctioning. He couldn't re-enter the house because the door connecting the house and garage locked when he pulled it shut. The family was on vacation. Mr. Side found himself locked in the garage for eight days. He subsisted on a case of Pepsi he found, and a large bag of dry dog food. He sued the homeowner's insurance claiming the situation caused him undue mental anguish. The jury agreed to the tune of half a million dollars.

The jury should have been locked in the garage with three insurance salesmen, overnight!

* * * * *

12
WORDS AND EXPRESSIONS

The basis of all comedy is the use of words and expressions. You hear great stuff not just from comics, but also from ordinary people, whether these are normal people on the street or someone at a board meeting. That is one reason why there can be a sequel to this book. Words are precisely what this chapter will be all about.

The expression, "Your call is important to us," is heard while we wait and wait and wait to talk to someone from customer service. But really, the phone call does have meaning for the business. That's why we are put on hold for a half hour or more. Someday when you are waiting and a voice finally comes on the line, just say, "Hold on, please."

*****

I'm sure you've heard the following phrase when you phoned some business in an attempt to get customer service. "We're sorry but at the present time all representatives are servicing a customer." On hearing this you may ask yourself, "Who is this person that is so special that everyone there is tending to him?" Maybe it's the Pope or the President.

*****

One manager might say to another person, "Al, we covered a lot of ground today." It sounds to me like these guys are part of the maintenance crew at Yankee Stadium, preparing the field for a game. I've heard another manager say, "She's got all the bases covered." Now tell me these people don't work at the ballpark! Another frequently used cliché that could have been borrowed from the sports world is "The whole nine yards." So are you planning to put carpet down in your living room?

*****

How about the boss who says, "I suggest strongly." Who does he think he is, Rocky Balboa? Another explanation might be that he hasn't taken a shower or a bath for a week or maybe he had garlic soup for lunch. Then again he may just have participated in a three-martini break and I need say no more. So perhaps the saying is appropriate.

*****

You have probably heard some sports enthusiast say, "This team is fired up!" Your friend may ask you to go to the game with him. He has an extra seat so he says to you, "I've got two dynamite seats at the game!" However, you think it over and say to him, "There is no way I am going to the game and sit in those seats if the team is 'fired up!'"

*****

Another phrase you hear way too much is "To tell you the truth" or "I'll be honest with you." You can curtail the use of this phrase very easily. Just respond, "Will that be for the rest of the day or just for the next few minutes?"

*****

I also have heard too many people say, "I guess what I think I'm saying is..." Be considerate and don't reply, "You haven't got a clue, have you?"

*****

Once in a while someone may ask you, "Do you see what I'm saying?" If anyone says this to you, just look around that person for a while and finally respond, "I'm looking but I don't see any captions."

*****

All too often you will hear someone from a bank say, "I'll cut you a check." I usually respond with the question, "Are you going to use scissors or a knife? How will I cash it if it's in two pieces?"

*****

You hear combinations of words that don't fit together, such as "required options." If it's an option, how can it be required? I have no idea what a "valid invoice error" is and we are bombarded with the term "bad debt." I guess some debts must be good, such as the national deficit.

*****

You have so often heard the statement after a terrorist attack that "the BPPO claimed 'responsibility' for the blast." In light of the happenings, I would think the operative word should be "irresponsibility."

*****

I've heard this expression on way too many Fridays, just before the weekend, "If I don't see you, have a nice weekend!" So then if you do see me, I should have a horrible weekend?

*****

A day won't pass when you haven't heard the following at least three times, "Have a nice day!" Usually people respond with, "You too." I have come up with a better reply. Just say, "Thanks, but I have other plans!"

*****

What about the expression, "I saw it with my own eyes." When I first pondered this saying, I wondered. However, now that many individuals are generous enough to donate their organs so that others can have a better life, I guess I have no argument.

*****

How many times have you heard someone say, "I know this woman who I'm sure you're going to like. I'll 'fix you up.'" At some time I may have no job and very few prospects. My friend might say, "Let's go out to dinner," to which I can only reply, "I'm broke." Well if "I'm broke," maybe I should get "fixed up!"

*****

You've heard the expression, "He comes from a broken home." I guess that's what you get for living in San Francisco. One of the features of that house is a sunken living room, although yesterday it wasn't. Talking about homes brings to mind real estate and the house on the lake with 3 bedrooms and 2 1/2 baths. Who are the people that need that 1/2 bath? Maybe it's good if you get a visit from your half brother. Then again it may just be the result of a broken home.

*****

At the dinner table, children tend to spend more time talking than eating and this may cause a father to say, "Keep your mouth shut until you are finished eating." Now, the youth to whom this is directed is caught on the horns of a dilemma (I was aware that many animals had horns but I never imagined them on a dilemma!) In order for anyone to eat dinner one must open one's mouth unless there is a new way of eating. At present this option is out of the question. So, if the child has to keep his mouth shut, how can he eat? To further complicate matters, the mother of the child chimes in with, "Hurry up and finish your supper." Now the poor kid is baffled on what to do.

*****

Here's an order I'm sure you've heard at the dinner table way too many times: "Don't play with your food!" With the new trends in gourmet cooking and eating, this saying could eventually be meaningful. After all, raw fish is very popular with all the sushi bars today and lobsters are cooked by placing a live crustacean into a pot of boiling water (if you're a lobster, ouch!) What about eating a live lobster? Now a child can play with his food and the lobster can play too. Each can enjoy the other's company.

A few days ago I was reminded of another expression from my childhood. I heard the remark, "He's not afraid to eat!" Well with that live lobster and his mean looking claws, I'm not surprised that any child would be terrified at the dinner table.

*****

Every parent has delivered this admonition to his offspring, "Don't get fresh!" You won't hear this phrase as often even though it certainly applies in many cases, "Don't be spoiled!" From these two expressions one may get the impression that kids have an expiration date, which is news to me.

*****

I heard someone say that they slept like a baby the night before. It wasn't too long before someone else said, "Yeah, he cried all night and wet the bed."

*****

If you worked in a meat department or your relatives were involved in a meat market, you probably heard the expression, "It's time to dress the chicken." If poultry, whether it be a turkey or a duck is dressed, is the attire formal, casual, business casual or costume casual? Maybe they're dressed for foul weather! And speaking of that fowl, I saw an advertisement somewhere for "turkey breast chops." Are turkeys now growing chops? They must look strange!

*****

Would you want a car that "runs like a top?" I certainly wouldn't, if it goes around in circles (sounds like a male who won't ask for directions when he's lost) and finally rolls over (the car and not the driver).

*****

You might hear someone say they just bought a personal computer with all the "bells and whistles." When they ask about my PC, I am so often tempted to say, "My printer has all the 'bells and whistles' too, and it drives me crazy when it's printing!"

*****

You hear this or a variation of this phrase all the time, "Drive carefully and get here in one piece." A bit later someone will say, "Joe's here. No wait, that's just part of him. I see the rest of him in the distance."

*****

What about all those yard sales that people have? You can never buy a "yard" at a yard sale and I'm sure that if you wish to purchase a barn, you won't be able to get one at a "barn sale." Then there's the garage sale, and it's the same story. The most challenging is trying to buy something at a "moving garage sale!"

*****

13
SOME QUESTIONS

We don't have all the answers to the mysteries of the universe. Many questions have yet to be answered, and here are a few. I am proud to say that I thought up some of these.

Why is the man who invests your money called a "broker?"

Why is the time of day with the slowest traffic called "rush hour?"

Why isn't there mouse-flavored cat food?

Can vegetarians eat animal crackers?

Is it true that cannibals don't eat clowns because they taste funny?

Why are there no "B" batteries?

Why do kamikaze pilots wear helmets?

When dog food has a new and improved taste, who tests it?

Why didn't Noah swat those two mosquitoes?

Why do they sterilize needles for lethal injections?

Why don't they make the whole airplane out of the material that makes up the black boxes?

Do sheep shrink when it rains?

Why are they called apartments when they are all stuck together?

If con is the opposite of pro, is Congress the opposite of progress?

If flying is so safe, why do they call the airport the terminal?

If Jimmy cracks corn and no one cares, why is there a song about him?

Why does an alarm clock go "off" when it actually turns on?

Why are they called stairs inside but steps outside?

If Milli Vanilli fell in the woods, would someone else make a sound?

If love is blind, how can anyone believe in love at first sight?

If the military uses "precision bombing," why do we have "collateral damage?"

Why is it that rain drops, but snow falls?

If the professor on Gilligan's Island can make a radio out of a coconut, why can't he fix a hole in the boat?

Why is it that "cargo" is transported by ship while a "shipment" is moved by car?

Why do we drive on the parkway but park in the driveway?

What was the best thing before sliced bread?

What's the opposite of "opposite?"

If you try to fail and succeed, what did you just do?

What do you call male ballerinas?

If there's only one person from Portugal in a room, is he a "Portugoose?"

Why do they call it getting your dog "fixed," if afterwards it doesn't work anymore?

Why is it when you tell someone there are a million stars in the universe, they believe you, but if you told them there's wet paint on the bench, they have to touch it?

If I play second base, third base and shortstop on a gas company or electric company baseball team, would I be a "utility player?"

Why is the alphabet song and "Twinkle Twinkle, Little Star" the same tune?

You can be overwhelmed and you can be underwhelmed, but can you just be "whelmed?"

Why do "fat chance" and "slim chance" mean the same thing?

Whose cruel idea was it to put an "s" in the word "lisp?"

Why are wrong phone numbers never busy?

Do people in Australia call the rest of the world, "up over?"

Does killing time damage eternity?

Why doesn't Tarzan have a beard?

Why is it that night falls, but day breaks?

Why is the third hand on a watch called a "second hand?"

Why is lemon juice made with artificial flavor but dishwashing liquid made with real lemons?

Are part-time bandleaders "semi-conductors?"

Can you buy an entire chess set in a pawnshop?

If we have daylight savings time, why are they saving it and where do they keep it?

Do jellyfish get gas from eating jellybeans?

Do fish get cramps after eating?

Do pilots take crash courses?

Why do they call it the Department of the Interior when they are in charge of everything outdoors?

How come Superman can stop bullets with his chest but always ducks when a gun is thrown at him?

Do stars clean themselves with meteor showers?

When they asked George Washington for ID, did he just whip out a quarter?

How much deeper would the ocean be if sponges didn't grow in it?

Have you ever imagined a world with no hypothetical situations?

Do they give you a parachute so you can get off a non-stop flight?

How do you write zero in Roman numerals?

How many weeks are there in a light year?

If a jogger runs at the speed of sound, can he still hear his Walkman?

If athletes get athletes foot, do astronauts get mistletoe?

If blind people wear sunglasses, why don't deaf people wear earmuffs?

If a deaf person swears, does his mother wash his hands with soap?

If cats and dogs didn't have fur, would we still pet them?

Why is "abbreviated" such a long word?

If space is a vacuum, who changes the bags?

Why do they lock gas station bathrooms? Are they afraid someone will clean them?

If you can't drink and drive, why do bars have parking lots?

If you spin a person from China or Japan around several times, will he become disoriented?

Why do signs that say "Slow Children" have a picture of a child running?

When sign makers go on strike, is anything written on their signs?

If someone with multiple personalities threatens to kill himself, is it considered a hostage situation?

Why do we sing "Take Me Out To The Ball Game," when we're already there?

What do you do when you see an endangered animal eating an endangered plant?

If a parsley farmer is sued, can they garnish his wages?

Why can't women put on mascara with their mouth closed?

Why don't we ever see the headline, "Psychic wins lottery?"

Why is it that to stop windows on your PC, you have to click "start?" If that wasn't ludicrous enough, to shut down my PC, I have to click "Start," then click "Turn Off Computer" and finally click "Turn Off." It's no wonder so many people are "turned off" by computers instead of the other way around.

If you fool around in a cave, can you get "hermit crabs?"

Is a head gasket used to fix a broken toilet?

Why is Chopin's Minute Waltz one minute and forty-three seconds? I thought musicians were good mathematicians.

Why do you see gasoline trucks filling up at a gas station? Shouldn't they be doing just the opposite?

What spices are used in seasoned firewood?

If you go to a covered dish supper, how do you eat (if all the dishes are covered?)?

Could a plastic surgeon also be called a "front end manager?"

Is a Polish neighborhood a "ski area?"

Does a plant manager need to have a degree in forestry?

Do they ever have a "gallop poll" at the racetrack?

Do the members of a standing committee get tired legs?

For whom is the sign at the post office which says, "For seeing eye dogs only?" It must be for the dogs! Is it true blind people don't skydive because it scares the hell out of the seeing eye dogs?

Are people who stand by the sports teams "athletic supporters?"

What effect does a leap year have on kangaroos?

You can be arrested if you are "legally drunk," but what if you are "illegally drunk?" What does that latter phrase mean anyway? Is it the result of drinking too much moonshine?

If I go to a department store, can I buy red tape?

If I am in a store that sells odds and ends and there is only one left, is it an odd or an end? If I go into any of these places and want the spread on any football game, will they give it to me?

If I am playing horseshoes and throw a ringer, why don't I hear bells? Maybe it's a dead ringer.

If they call the NCAA basketball tournament, "March Madness," why are the last three games usually in April?

Would Heidi Fleiss be the person who should be in charge of corporate affairs?

If I am about to write a check to Roseanne Cash, can I say to her, "Should I make that payable to 'cash?' or would that be redundant?"

If we get a "new lease on life", from whom do we get it? From God, I hope. But where do we send the mortgage payments? How long will the lease last and can we afford the payments? What if there is something in the lease we don't like?

Do you get generic cancer from generic cigarettes?

Are there delis in New Delhi?

Was a "singing telegram" the first "voice mail?"

Would you stop to eat at a place with the sign, "Eat here——get gas?"

If I am spying on the enemy on patrol, won't he see the reflection on the glass of my binoculars? However, if I smear mud on them, how can I see anything?

If after final exams, teachers are pressed for time, can they take their papers to be graded at the Attica Correctional Institute?

Do the guys in prison have "cell phones?" They must. If not, how else can they keep going with all their drug business?

Who sharpens the bullets for sharpshooters? It is rather ironic that slang for a gun is "piece" while the word "peace" represents a state of tranquility.

Can I make a dry martini with "dry ice?" If an area is a so-called "dry county", can the people there drink "Bud Dry?"

Will it be healthier if you have an ice cream sandwich on whole wheat?

If a veteran of World War II who lost one of his legs in battle needs a garment for his bottom torso, does he buy a "pant?"

Why do we put suits in a garment bag and garments in a suitcase?

Does the shortest day of the year have only twenty-three hours?

If I drive a sub-compact car and wind up in a collision that demolishes the vehicle, would it be sub-totaled?

Are you in the wrong church if the person at the pulpit does a reading from the book of "suburbs?"

When someone asks "not to be named," isn't it a bit too late?

What happens when a splinter group runs out of toothpicks?

If someone is calling in a bomb threat and they get voice mail, do they leave a message?

Is a "staff meeting" only intended for shepherds? Maybe the only people in attendance should be the music teachers.

What do little birdies see when they get knocked unconscious?

Is it true that people on a steering committee always come to work in car pools? And why is it called a "carpool" since there isn't any water in the car and certainly not enough room for a pool table?

Regarding "legal briefs," do lawyers wear underwear that is different from normal people?

If I'm "put through the wringer," should the setting be permanent press?

Is the opposite of "increment," "excrement?"

Is a "brief rundown" the fatigue you feel because your jockey shorts are too tight?

If a house arrest takes place and I am not at home, will I be safe?

If a Latin American country has a dictator, does he have a secretary to take shorthand?

Going further east, if Hussein of Iraq had imposed his rule on Kuwait, could you say that the country was "Saddamized?"

Do they sing "Guantanamera" at Guantanamo Bay?

If workers get a floating holiday, do they go on a weekend cruise?

If lawyers are disbarred and clergymen defrocked, doesn't it follow that electricians can be delighted, musicians denoted, cowboys deranged, models deposed, tree surgeons debarked and dry cleaners depressed?

If Fed Ex and UPS were to merge, would they call it Fed UP?

Do Lipton Tea employees take coffee breaks?

If it's true that we are here to help others, then what exactly are the others here for?

Whatever happened to Preparations A through G?

Could the entire world smoke a "universal joint?"

If four out of five people suffer from diarrhea, does that mean that one enjoys it?

If people from Poland are called Poles, why aren't people from Holland called Holes?

Why is a person who plays the piano called a pianist but a person who drives a racecar not called a racist?

If a restaurant has a sign, "2 eggs, any style," does that include "gangland style?" I think I'll order either the "Elizabethan style" or "Gothic style."

Do you get cold cash because someone at the bank put a freeze on your funds?

If I receive mail and on the envelope there is writing that says, "Time Sensitive material," is there a bomb inside?

The next three questions must be credited to the CBC program, "Royal Canadian Air Farce."

Is it fair for a police officer to ask a gay drunk to walk a straight line?

If a tree falls on Forrest Whitaker, does he make a sound?

If rice is in Rice Krispies, and wheat is in Wheaties, what's in Cap'N Crunch?

Well, I've just about run out of interesting nuggets of intelligence. Because of all that is happening daily in our world, there is a good chance of a sequel. I added these last few words so that no one is left "up in the air." Nor did I want to "leave you hanging." This brings me to the final question.

Isn't it cruel to leave someone with vertigo "out on a limb?"

References and Recommended Reading

Daniel Butler, Alan Rey with Larry Rose - Crimes And Misdumbmeanors (1998: Rutledge Hill Press - Nashville)

Al Franken - Lies and the Lying Liars Who Tell Them (2003: Dutton - New York)

Thomas Friedman - From Beirut To Jerusalem (1989: Farrar, Straus, Giroux - New York)

Leland H. Gregory III - Great Government Goofs (1997: Bantam, Doubleday & Dell - New York)

Jim Hightower - Let's Stop Beating Around the Bush (2004: Viking Press - New York)

Molly Ivins - Molly Ivins Can't Say That, Can She? (1991: Random House - New York)

Gus Russo - Live By The Sword: The Secret War Against Castro And The Death Of JFK (1998: Bancroft Press - Baltimore)

Helen Thomas - Thanks for the Memories, Mr. President (2002: Scribner - New York)